FROM FISHERMAN'S WHARF TO STEINBECK'S CANNERY ROW

A Pictorial History of
Monterey's Historic Waterfront
and Its Famed Sardine Industry

FROM FISHERMAN'S WHARF TO STEINBECK'S CANNERY ROW

A Pictorial History of Monterey's Historic Waterfront and Its Famed Sardine Industry

Randall A. Reinstedt

Ghost Town Publications
Carmel, California
www.ghosttownpub.com

For other books by Randall A. Reinstedt, see page 203. If book-stores in your area do not carry these titles, copies may be ordered by writing to . . .

**Ghost Town Publications
P.O. Drawer 5998
Carmel, CA 93921**

Or visit our web site:

www.ghosttownpub.com

10 9 8 7 6 5 4 3 2 1

Manufactured in the United States of America

ISBN 978-0-933818-14-9
Library of Congress Control Number: 2008940057

Edited by John Bergez
Typesetting by Erick and Mary Ann Reinstedt
Cover and illustrated maps by Ed Greco

This book is dedicated to the fisherfolk,
and to all who had a part in making Monterey
the Sardine Capital of the World

Preface

This book was originally published in 1978 as *Where Have All the Sardines Gone?* I am happy to say it was well received by members of the fishing community and all who were involved in making Monterey "The Sardine Capital of the World." Yes, in the early to mid 1970s—when I was busy tracking down the veteran fisherfolk and collecting their stories—not only were many of them still a part of the waterfront scene (often gathering in small groups along Cannery Row and on the wharves), but they enjoyed talking about the days of the sardine and the parts they and their extended families played in making Monterey one of the world's major fishing ports.

Thirty-plus years later, as I'm in the process of expanding, updating, and rewriting this text, many of the aged fishermen and ex-cannery workers have died, and much of the Monterey waterfront as they knew it has also passed from the scene. Certainly, Fisherman's Wharf retains its charm and remains one of the Pacific Coast's most picturesque piers. Parts of Cannery Row, too, are reminiscent of a time that was, with Doc's Lab and the old Wing Chong Market—both of which were immortalized in John Steinbeck's novel *Cannery Row*—being among the most recognizable buildings of the sardine/Steinbeck era. But one event—more than any other—has put the Monterey waterfront back on the map: the opening of the fabulous Monterey Bay Aquarium in 1984.

Located at the north end of Cannery Row, where the Hovden Cannery once stood (with the shell of the old cannery having been incorporated into its design), the aquarium straddles the line that divides the communities of Monterey and Pacific Grove. In a relatively short time it has gained international fame as one of the best facilities of its kind in the world and made Cannery Row the number-one tourist attraction on the Monterey Peninsula.

The phenomenal success of the aquarium, and the changes it has helped bring about on old Cannery Row, are among the many reasons I chose to expand this work and republish it under a new title. In 1978 the title *Where Have All the Sardines Gone?* spoke eloquently to many residents and visitors who were keenly aware of Monterey's fishing heritage and the devastating effect that the disappearance of the sardine had on the Peninsula's economy. But as time has marched on, fewer and fewer people remember the passing of the sardine industry or the canneries that gave the Row its name. It was with such things in mind that I decided it was time for a change of title along with the updates I planned for the book. While much of the text remains largely the same, briefly telling the story of the rise and fall of the sardine industry, a new section of photographs focusing on the Monterey Bay Aquarium's first twenty-five years has been added at the end of the book. These pictures, along with numerous new photos that have been added to "The Story in Pictures" section, will provide future readers with a more accurate look at the Monterey waterfront, its fishing industry, and world-famous Cannery Row.

Randall A. Reinstedt

Contents

FROM FISHERMAN'S WHARF TO STEINBECK'S CANNERY ROW

A Pictorial History of
Monterey's Historic Waterfront
and Its Famed Sardine Industry

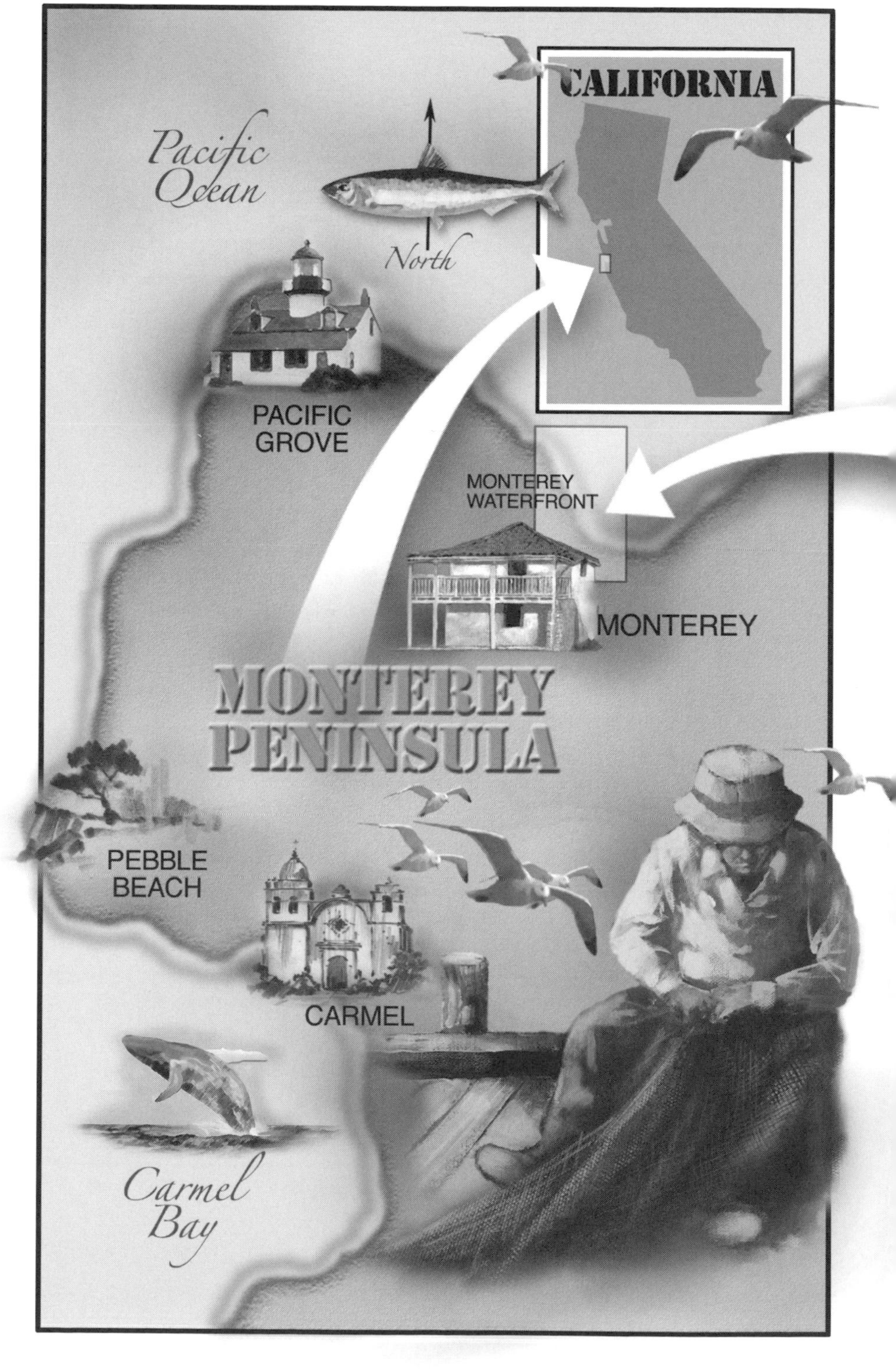

Pacific
Ocean

North

PACIFIC
GROVE

CALIFORNIA

MONTEREY
WATERFRONT

MONTEREY

MONTEREY
PENINSULA

PEBBLE
BEACH

CARMEL

Carmel
Bay

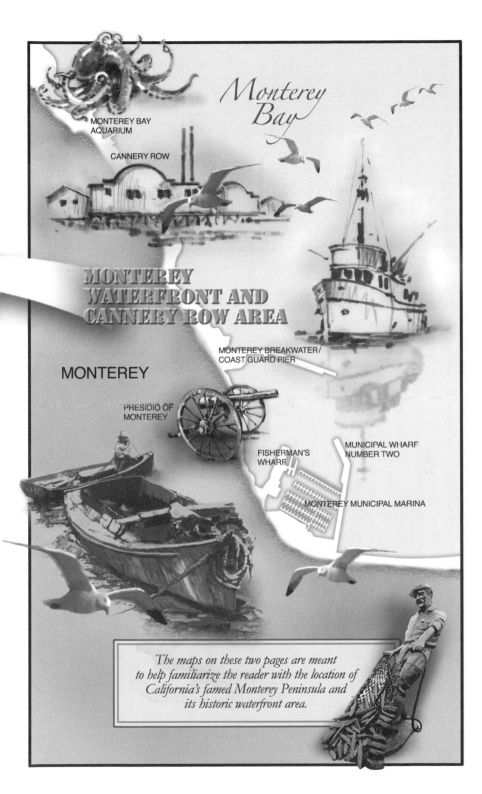

Monterey Bay

MONTEREY BAY AQUARIUM

CANNERY ROW

MONTEREY WATERFRONT AND CANNERY ROW AREA

MONTEREY BREAKWATER/ COAST GUARD PIER

MONTEREY

PRESIDIO OF MONTEREY

MUNICIPAL WHARF NUMBER TWO

FISHERMAN'S WHARF

MONTEREY MUNICIPAL MARINA

The maps on these two pages are meant to help familiarize the reader with the location of California's famed Monterey Peninsula and its historic waterfront area.

CANNERY ROW – 1946

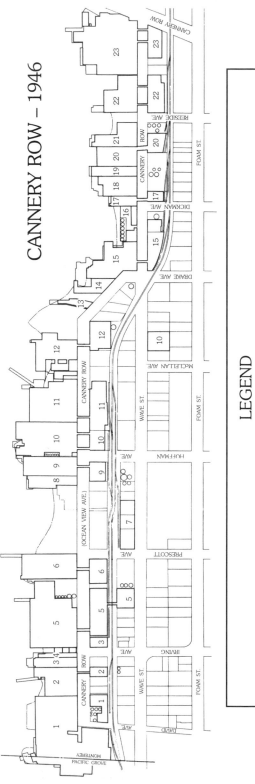

LEGEND

1. Hovden Food Products Corp.
2. Atlantic Coast Fisheries Co.
3. Monterey Fish Products, Inc.
4. Del Vista Packing Co.
5. Del Mar Canning Co.
6. Monterey Canning Co.
7. Edgewater Packing Co.
8. Sea Beach Packing Co.
9. Custom House Packing Corp.
10. Carmel Canning Co.
11. California Packing Corp.
12. San Xavier Fish Packing Co.
13. Western Sardine Co., Inc.
14. Ferrante Co.
15. Oxnard Canners, Inc.
16. Western Fish Products Corp.
17. Aenas Sardine Packing Co.
18. Central Packing Co.
19. Ronada Fisheries & Manola Packing Co.
20. Enterprise Packers
21. California Frozen Fish Co.
22. Peninsula Packing Co.
23. San Carlos Canning Co.

Courtesy of California History Room Archives, Monterey Public Library

Introduction

This publication tells the story of Monterey's waterfront and its famed sardine industry. Of course, in a volume of this size it is impossible to tell the whole story, or to adequately give credit to the countless people and events that played a part in bringing the title of "The Sardine Capital of the World" to this bayside community. With this in mind the text portion of the book is admittedly brief. Among the historic highlights it touches upon are the sardine industry's early years, when men like Frank E. Booth, Knute Hovden, and Pietro "Pete" Ferrante helped bring international fame to this modest-sized port city. The story continues with the development of Cannery Row, including the part John Steinbeck played in preserving the street's colorful past as well as the coming of the Monterey Bay Aquarium. In these pages you will also find information about the waterfront's picturesque wharves, the introduction of the purse seiner, the seasons of 200,000-ton catches, the disappearance (and recent reappearance) of the sardine, and the hardships and heartaches experienced by the hardy fisherfolk who are the true heroes of the tale.

In planning this book it was my desire to let the pictures tell the story. Firmly believing in the adage that a picture is worth a thousand words, I spent several years gathering photographs that I thought would do justice to both the industry and its people. In providing context for these images, I have taken great pains to ensure the captions are as accurate as possible. Nevertheless, with much of the information coming from aged, and perhaps exaggerated, newspaper accounts, along with the faded memories of old-timers, it would be unrealistic to assume that each and every name, date, or figure is beyond question. For this reason I would like to apologize in advance for any inadvertent errors or omissions.

With that said, I hope that this book will be accepted for what it was meant to be—a pictorial history of the Monterey waterfront and its famed fishing industry—and that it will be enjoyed by all who read it, especially the families of the hard-working fisherfolk who cherish their memories and who still call Monterey home.

A Brief History of
the Monterey Waterfront

Monterey by the Bay

For some the history of Monterey had its start in the long-ago year of 1542. It was in that year that historians credit the Portuguese navigator Juan Rodríguez Cabrillo with being the first European to spot its rounded bay. Others, admittedly only a few, credit the privateer Francis Drake with being the first European to actually set foot on the Monterey Peninsula. They therefore claim Monterey's history should begin with the English adventurer's (disputed) visit in 1579. Then there are those who believe the naming of Monterey Bay in 1602 by the Spanish explorer Sebastián Vizcaíno launched the history of the bayside town. Finally, aficionados of California's mission period point to 1770 as the year the modern history of the Monterey Peninsula began. It was then that the diminutive Franciscan Padre Junípero Serra, the head of California's famed mission chain, met his military commander, Gaspar de Portolá, on the Monterey shore and founded what was to become California's first capital city. Among the other items of historic significance that took place at this meeting were the founding of the Presidio of Monterey and the mission that would become Serra's headquarters. Originally located on the Presidio grounds, the mission was moved "over the hill" to its present Carmel site in 1771. There Serra lived, died, and was buried. Known today as Carmel Mission, the church is often described as the most beautiful and historic of California's twenty-one missions.

From this point on, countless events helped to make Monterey the unique and history-rich community it is today. For example, in 1818 the Pacific privateer Hippolyte de Bouchard attacked the capital city, making Monterey the only California town to have been sacked by a "pirate." (Although several sources suggest Bouchard was more a privateer than a pirate, most agree that the events that took place on this occasion were indeed acts of piracy.) In 1822 Mexico gained its independence from Spain, with Monterey retaining its capital city status. In the 1840s Monterey was twice attacked by gunboats flying the red, white, and blue. While both attacks were successful, it wasn't until 1846 that the Americans planted their roots. With the second raising of the Stars and Stripes, this time by Commodore John Drake Sloat, much of what we now know as the southwestern United States came under American rule. Three years later, Monterey hosted California's first constitutional convention, paving the way for California's entrance into the Union as the thirty-first state in 1850.

During the next two decades Monterey was perhaps best known as a whaling port. In 1874 California's first narrow-gauge railroad chugged into town. Then, with the dawn of the 1880s, a new kind of fame was bestowed upon the community as travelers from many distant lands began flocking to the fabulous Hotel Del Monte, which had opened its doors on the bay's south shore. Described as "the most elegant seaside establishment in the world," the Del Monte hosted celebrities from across the globe. As the fame of the facility continued to spread, the Del Monte, and with it the Monterey Peninsula, became the place to see and be seen by the wealthy of the world.

In the turn-of-the-century year of 1900, a man named Frank E. Booth moved to Monterey. Booth had been a frequent visitor to the area long before his move and had consistently been impressed by the number of sardines that abounded in the bay. At the time of his trips to the Peninsula, Booth and his father were involved in the canning of salmon in their Pittsburg, California, plant. This background prompted the younger Booth to ponder the possibility of canning the abundant Monterey Bay sardine. The founding of the F. E. Booth Company in a plant near Monterey's old Custom House soon followed. (The Custom House, circa 1820s, is one of California's most historic structures. It is located across from the entrance to Fisherman's Wharf.) The founding of the Booth Company, and the building of the plant, are often described as the beginning of Monterey's sardine industry.

Not long after Booth launched the California sardine as a commercially canned product, a second man arrived on the scene who, along with Booth, was destined to become an important figure in Monterey's multimillion-dollar sardine industry. Knute Hovden was a recent immigrant from Norway, a graduate of the Norwegian National Fisheries College, and a skillfully trained professional in the fish-packing field. He soon teamed up with Booth, and it was through the efforts of these two visionaries that the highly competitive, and extremely profitable, Monterey sardine industry continued to develop and expand.

9

With Booth and Hovden perfecting the canning phase of the industry, the time soon came when the biggest problem they faced was securing a steady supply of fish. With the ability to process five tons of sardines per day, and with the daily catch being highly erratic (due, in part, to the fishing methods that were currently in use, combined with the questionable skill of many of the local fishermen), Booth and Hovden decided that their next project would be to find a way to increase, and ensure, the size of the daily catch.

A Man Called Pete

At this point a man who was to become one of Monterey's best-known and most respected citizens arrived on the scene. Pietro Ferrante, born on the island of Sicily in 1867, and affectionately called Pete by all who knew him, was this man.

By the time Pete Ferrante arrived in Monterey in 1904, he had many years of fishing experience behind him and had gained a reputation as a man of vision and considerable fishing skill. With Booth, Hovden, and Ferrante all in the area at the same time, and all realizing the untapped potential of the Monterey Bay sardine, it was only natural that they would soon get together.

The bust of Pietro Ferrante occupies a place of honor near the entrance of Fisherman's Wharf. *Reinstedt photo & Collection*

After observing the methods of fishing that were being used, Ferrante voiced the opinion that a new approach to the catching of sardines was needed if they were to truly reap the bounty of the bay. Thinking back to the lampara boat and net method of fishing he had been familiar with as a boy in the Mediterranean, Ferrante began to redesign the lampara net and adapt it for use in the deep-water bay of Monterey. (The word *lampara* was derived from the Italian word *lampo*, meaning lightning, because the net was designed for a fast cast and haul. A lampara net is capable of encircling an entire school of fish. This enables the fishermen to bring the whole catch to the lampara boat, where it can be taken from the sea.)

After demonstrating the practicality of the lampara net to a gathering of local skeptics—including many Monterey fishermen—and after being given the go-ahead by Booth, Ferrante sent word to his Italian fishermen friends in Sicily, Pittsburg, and along California's Sacramento River, urging them to come to Monterey and join him in the hunt for sardines. Heeding the call, many of Ferrante's friends and relatives ventured to the rounded bay.

As has been stated so often, it was the arrival of the skilled Italian fishermen that started Monterey on its way to becoming a major fishing port. Indeed, most sources credit Pietro Ferrante with being the father of Monterey's famed fishing fraternity. In fairness to all, however, it should be noted that many other pioneer fishermen also played an important part in the early development of Monterey's fishing industry.

A Change of Scenes

With the aid of the lampara net, and with the knowledge and skill of the newly arrived fishermen, Monterey began to experience a gradual but significant change. By 1913 the canning industry, with its carefully developed techniques and modernized mode of operation, had come of age, and was no longer looked upon as being in the crude and experimental stage. In keeping up with the canners, the fishing boat crews, which usually consisted of six highly trained workers, were catching as much as twenty-five tons of sardines in a single night. (Those unfamiliar with the techniques used by the sardine fishermen may be surprised to learn that the ideal fishing conditions were on dark, moonless nights. It was then that the fishermen could best spot the phosphorescent glow of a school of sardines and know where to place their nets.)

With the supply of fish no longer a problem, Knute Hovden decided to branch out on his own. In 1916 he opened a cannery on a stretch of beach near the north end of what is now Cannery Row. History buffs might be interested in knowing that a large Chinese fishing village was once located in this area. In 1888 the United States Commission of Fish and Fisheries described the village as "one of the most thriving settlements of its kind on the West Coast."

Sadly, the village was destroyed by fire in 1906. Today the Monterey Bay Aquarium occupies part of this site.

With others following Hovden's move, the shoreline soon became lined with several noisy, smelly, smoke-belching canneries. By 1918 Monterey boasted a total of nine such complexes (many of them located along the shore between the Booth and Hovden plants) and packed a total of 1,400,000 cases of sardines, compared to a mere 75,000 cases a short three years before. At this point in local history, people did not concern themselves with saving scenic shorelines. As a result, it was not long before this once picturesque stretch of Monterey beach was lost to industry, progress, and the overabundant sardine.

The early 1920s were the peak years of the lampara boat and net method of fishing, as 1925 brought the introduction of the half-ring net. Over the years the lampara boats had increased in size along with their specially designed lighters (tow barges in which to haul their catch). Rather than being small and awkward, as many of their predecessors had been, the newer boats reached lengths of forty feet and boasted trim lines as well as dependable motors.

With the introduction of the half-ring net, the half-ring boat also appeared. This craft differed only slightly from the lampara boat as, among other things, it boasted a winch, a mast, and a boom. With the use of the rings, from which the half-ring net and boat got their names, many more fish could be caught per haul as the net rings pursed (or pocketed) the net, thus trapping the fish and making it difficult for them to escape.

The Sardine Capital of the World

Within a few years the lampara boat, as well as the more efficient half-ring craft, became outmoded with the introduction of a vessel bearing a name that at one time was almost synonymous with the name Monterey: the purse seiner. This popular vessel took its name from the type of net, or seine, it carried, which, when full of fish, formed a purse.

The purse seiners varied in size. The largest approached one hundred feet in length and carried nets that were wide enough to encircle a football field and could be dropped to a depth equaling the height of a ten-story building. This new breed of boat was also capable of fishing more than one hundred miles at sea and carrying two hundred tons of fish in its hold. With the introduction of the purse seiner, and the elimination of the lighter, sardine fishing in and around the Monterey Bay area took on an added dimension.

Through the thirties and early forties the Monterey fishing fleet and its supporting cast of canneries continued to grow and prosper. In 1930 the catch was 159,000 tons. By 1935 it had jumped to 230,000 tons, and during the early 1940s there were years when the catch approached the almost unbelievable figure of a quarter of a million tons of sardines!

With the supply of fish being both constant and abundant, cannery operators had long since learned that there was money to be made not only in the canning of fish but in the processing of fish by-products as well. Fish meal was becoming widely used for poultry and livestock feed, as well as being in demand for use as fertilizer. The oil from the fish—which at one time was considered waste—was sought after in the manufacture of soap, paint mixer, vitamins, glycerin (for ammunition), shortening, salad oil, and the tanning of leather. By 1945 (considered by many the zenith year of the local fishing industry), Monterey boasted nineteen canneries and twenty reduction plants for the development of fish by-products. The fishing fleet numbered well over one hundred, with eighty-four of the vessels being of the purse seiner variety. It was during this period that Monterey was known as the Sardine Capital of the World. In total tonnage it ranked third among the world's major fishing ports (with Stavanger, Norway, and Hull, England, ranked one and two).

A Tale of Inches

To illustrate the enormous number of sardines that were delivered to Cannery Row during a good year, a tale of inches (with the *Monterey Peninsula Herald* providing the statistics) proves effective. The year 1939 boasted a catch of some 215,000 tons, or 430,000,000 pounds, of sardines. With the 1939 catch averaging approximately three fish to the pound, this translates into 1,290,000,000 sardines! As staggering as this number is, the following figures are even more amazing.

Assuming the average length of the sardine caught during the 1939 season to be ten inches (although many were considerably larger), the combined length of the year's catch comes to 12,900,000,000 inches. To put this astronomical number into perspective, imagine the sardines laid end to end. The line of fish would stretch a distance of approximately 203,600 miles—or nearly the distance from Earth to the moon!

Carrying this project one step further, we find that if our row of ten-inch sardines (which would be a bit smelly by now) were laid end to end in a line that stretched around the world at the equator, they would circle Earth eight times . . . with over 3,600 miles of fish left over!

All Was Not Glory

Even as Monterey's sardine industry continued to grow and prosper, there were many minuses that had to be counted along with the pluses. As early as 1903, when the sardine industry was just getting its start, the F. E. Booth canning plant mysteriously burned down. The blame for the catastrophe fell on local fishermen who were described as disliking Booth, his sardines, and the smell of his cannery. Undaunted by the fire, Booth resumed operations in a nearby smokehouse. Upon opening a saloon adjacent to the smokehouse, the enterprising Booth served fish along with schooners of beer. From that point on Booth's sardines were known locally as "soused mackerel."

As the years rolled on, other fires struck, destroying numerous canneries and warehouses in the process. Some say the worst conflagration occurred in 1951. In that year the Westgate-Sun Harbor complex went up in flames. Approximately $1,500,000 worth of canned fish was destroyed, leading the event to be listed as the third largest food fire in United States history.

If it wasn't fires destroying canneries, it was unpredictable storms unleashing their fury on the fleet (with the storms of 1915, 1919, 1943, and 1953 being among the worst on record). Even during the "good times" when no fires or storms caused heartache or grief, there were the dreaded recessions that caused canneries to change hands or go bankrupt. To add to the woe of the canners and fishermen, a sizable group of locals (mainly residents and merchants who were not dependent upon the sardine for survival) annually complained to city hall about the odors and pollution created by the canneries and the reduction plants. Problems within the industry itself also created considerable difficulties, as each year boat owners, fishermen, cannery owners, and cannery workers somehow had to be brought together in an agreement on wages. The negotiations were complicated by the fact that they revolved around the projected availability of the sardine. The animated discussions and countless meetings became a yearly ritual along the waterfront, usually accompanied by considerable fist waving and the burning of much midnight oil. Skullduggery was also an unfortunate part of the scene, as among other underhanded schemes, deals were sometimes made between boat owners and canners whereby over-limit catches were overlooked.

Certainly I could go on listing the problems and frustrations of Monterey's sardine industry, but as one old-timer aptly put it, "Why pop a bubble that has already burst?"

Where Have All the Sardines Gone?

The year 1945 is remembered as the high point of Monterey's sardine industry, as the beginning of the low point for the industry came the very next year. Although fish continued to be caught and canneries continued to work, the handwriting was on the wall for all to see. The 1946 catch was nearly 100,000 tons under the 1945 mark, and the 1947 catch was more than 100,000 tons less than that. The 1948 catch plummeted to a disastrous 14,000 tons, with much of even that amount being trucked to the Monterey canneries from more abundant fishing grounds to the south.

As the cash flow from the previously prosperous sardine industry dropped to a mere trickle, people and businesses throughout the Peninsula felt the pinch. Then, with optimism at its low point, the industry—for unknown reasons—received a welcome shot in the arm in 1949 as the catch rebounded to 41,000 tons. As the 1950 season rolled around, thousands of Peninsulans crossed their fingers, praying that the unpredictable sardine would once again return to central California waters. As if bowing to their wishes, the sardine arrived on schedule, enabling the fleet to record a catch of 132,000 tons! Even though this was more than 100,000 tons less than the catch of 1945, the industry's dollar turnover was the greatest in its history.

Yet, as the 1950 season came to a close, for all intents and purposes so too did Monterey's sardine industry. The 1951 catch was embarrassingly small, and by 1952 canneries were folding at such a rapid rate that only brief mentions of their closings made the local papers.

As the canneries closed (with many selling their equipment at a fraction of its original cost to canneries in such distant places as Venezuela and South Africa), many of the purse seiners found their way to various southland ports where sardines were still frolicking in the sea. With the harbor relatively empty of purse seiners, and much of Cannery Row on the auction block, Monterey's sardine industry became little more than a memory. Millions had been made during the rowdy and robust days of the sardine, and millions had been lost as the industry went from boom to bust in less than half a century. As people looked back at the color and pageantry of old Monterey's sardine industry, the haunting question "Where have all the sardines gone?" remained a mystery to many. Some shook their heads and talked about polluted waters, warmer climates, changes in currents, and recurring cycles. Others pointed to the distinct possibility that the once-abundant sardine was just plain fished out.

Along Came John

Even though the bubble that was Monterey's mighty sardine industry began to burst after the peak season of 1945, a second chapter in life along the Monterey waterfront began to take shape in that very same year. Among the events that marked 1945 as a year to remember on the Peninsula was the publication of a book called *Cannery Row*. This classic novel was written by the Salinas-born author John Steinbeck. (The city of Salinas lies about twenty miles to the northeast of Monterey. Steinbeck, of course, was one of America's best-known authors and a winner of both the Nobel and Pulitzer prizes.) Steinbeck's story of the color and characters along what was then Ocean View Avenue became so popular, and focused so much attention on the mile-long stretch of corrugated metal, tilted smoke stacks, and eye-catching walkways high above the street, that in 1958 the city of Monterey officially changed the name of the cannery-lined street to Cannery Row.

With Steinbeck's book immortalizing the Row as "a poem, a stink, a grating noise, a quality of light, a tone, a habit, a nostalgia, a dream," it was inevitable that the curious would come to see for themselves. Such landmark sites as Doc's Lab, Wing Chong's Market, the overgrown lot where Mack and the boys dreamed the days away, and, of course, the popular Lone Star, where Flora and the girls practiced the oldest profession, all became known and revered sites to lovers of Steinbeck lore. With the tourists coming in ever increasing numbers, and the sardines staying away in equally increasing numbers (the comeback years of 1949 and 1950 being the exceptions),

From Steinbeck Plaza, in the heart of Cannery Row, John continues to watch over the street he helped to make famous. *R. Reinstedt photo & Collection*

the business-oriented people of Monterey began looking toward the silver of the coins dispensed by the visitors rather than the silver of the sardine that for so many years had meant prosperity and security to the people of the Peninsula.

There Is More to the Waterfront Than Old Cannery Row

As fascinating to many as Cannery Row is Monterey's popular and picturesque Fisherman's Wharf. The story of Fisherman's Wharf (as well as the city's other docks and piers) is an interesting chapter in Monterey's history.

To fully appreciate the growth of the Monterey waterfront, one must look back to the year 1845. It was in this year that Thomas O. Larkin (the United States consul to Mexican-ruled California) decided it was time that Alta (Upper) California's capital city had a wharf. Thinking it inappropriate that visitors arriving by sea should be forced to jump from launches and wade through breakers in their efforts to reach the shore, and fully aware that docking facilities would help immeasurably with the loading and unloading of merchandise from his nearby store, the industrious Larkin decided to finance the construction of a pier.

The completion of this structure enabled Monterey to claim California's first wharf. Located in the vicinity of the present day Fisherman's Wharf, Larkin's 1845 pier stretched only a short distance into the sea. It cost its builder an estimated $8,000, with aged accounts stating Larkin paid $1,500 for 1,500 cartloads of rock and $4 for each wooden piling.

Records are somewhat vague as to what became of Larkin's pier, as the next mention of wharves along the Monterey waterfront states that in 1868 the Pacific Coast Steamship Company began construction of a second wharf "where the first once stood." Completed in 1870, the Steamship Company pier was four hundred feet long and boasted a freight warehouse and Steamship Company office at its seaward end. Upon its completion the Pacific Coast Steamship Company inaugurated a freight and passenger service to Monterey, with ships calling at the new facility four times per week.

In 1874 Monterey was blessed with a second pier and a railroad as well. The coming of the railroad was another important first for the former capital city, as the newly formed Monterey and Salinas Valley Railroad Company was the first narrow-gauge railroad to be built in the state.

Upon completion of the railroad the company built a 1,300-foot pier in front of its depot (where the Monterey Marina is now located). Although the railroad was relatively short-lived (eventually bowing to the mighty Southern Pacific), its pier remained intact (with periodic repairs and rebuilding) until it was removed in 1940.

In later years other piers, such as the Bathhouse pier of the famed Hotel Del Monte, the Booth Cannery pier, and the Coalinga Oil and Transportation Company Wharf (better known as the Associated Oil Company pier), were built in and about the Monterey waterfront. Even though each of the piers served a purpose and hummed with activity, the original Pacific Coast Steamship Company wharf remained the center of harbor life for the people of Monterey.

18

A Change of Names and a Change of Scenes

In 1913, with the sardine fishing industry continuing to expand, and the desire to keep the Steamship Company pier in better repair, the City of Monterey assumed ownership of the aging wharf. It was during this period that the Steamship Company pier became known as Fisherman's Wharf.

After leasing space to defray upkeep costs and to help finance additions, the city added a wing for freighter service in 1917. By 1920 the wharf boasted several warehouses, approximately twenty wholesale and retail fish outlets, a restaurant, a marine service station, and an abalone-shell grinding business.

In March of 1923, with the Monterey wharf stacked high with 20,000 cases of sardines (the largest load of sardines ever to have been shipped from the port), disaster struck in the form of bad weather. As the steamship *San Antonio* awaited the loading of her cargo, swells and waves from the open bay caused her to lean too heavily on the wharf. This resulted in the collapse of a 132-foot section of the pier. As the pier gave in to the crunch of the *San Antonio,* 9,750 cases of sardines slid into the bay!

With nearly half of the $200,000 sardine payload in the choppy waters of the bay, local fishermen were summoned to salvage what they could. Working as if their lives depended on each and every case they could recover, the hardworking fishermen succeeded in bringing 4,000 cases of "recaught" sardines back to the pier. An additional 5,000 cases were salvaged by divers. Thanks to these extraordinary efforts, the final loss totaled only 750 cases.

In the construction that followed, the 400-foot length of the original Steamship Company pier was extended an additional 750 feet. A marine service station and a finger pier to the east were added at this time.

The year 1925 brought a new look to the Monterey waterfront in the form of a second, and much longer, municipal wharf. Built to the east of Fisherman's Wharf and the Monterey and Salinas Valley Railroad Company pier, and extending approximately 1,700 feet into the bay, "Wharf Number Two" was an important addition to the waterfront, as it aptly met the needs of the expanding commercial fishing industry. Completed on December 31, 1926 (at a cost of $246,000), the new wharf served many purposes, including that of a cargo pier, and helped immeasurably in relieving congestion in and around Fisherman's Wharf.

In the fall of 1931 construction began on Monterey's long overdue breakwater. Like Wharf Number Two, the new breakwater stretched approximately 1,700 feet into the sea. Upon its completion in 1934, the harbor became a much more sheltered refuge for its ever-expanding fishing fleet. Unfortunately, as is illustrated on pages 123–125, the completion of the breakwater didn't completely solve the problems of fierce ocean winds and unpredictable Pacific storms.

Remember the People

Over half a century has passed since the corrugated canneries along the Row and the sleek purse seiners anchored in the bay last brought prosperity to the people of the Monterey Peninsula. Much of Cannery Row and the downtown Monterey waterfront has been transformed into a multitude of visitor-oriented businesses and convention facilities. This is not to say that remnants of the old Row don't still exist, or that Fisherman's Wharf doesn't remind one of a time that was. Yes, the Monterey of today—as was the case prior to the sardine, when the Hotel Del Monte was the talk of the land—once again relies on its visitors to stimulate its economy. Perhaps this is as it should be, as the Monterey Peninsula has been richly blessed and has much to offer both visitors and residents.

Among its many blessings, and one of more recent vintage, is the Monterey Bay Aquarium. Opened in 1984, this world-renowned facility not only has been a boon to Monterey but has helped stimulate the economy of the whole Peninsula. As one would expect, with its unprecedented success other businesses were to follow, and today, as in days of old, Cannery Row again bustles with activity.

Elsewhere on the waterfront, there is even a modest revival of sardine fishing. Yes, the sardines are back—enough of them, at least, to make sardine fishing worthwhile for a small number of boat owners based in Monterey and nearby Moss Landing. As the *Monterey County Herald* reported in July, 2008, today sardine fishing is heavily regulated to protect the stocks of the silvery fish. And so it is that some hardy captains and crews are once again venturing into the waters near Monterey in quest of sardines. As one of them said, "It's been my dream all my life to fish for sardines in Monterey. I stood out there on the boat the other night and said, 'This is just like when my grandfather was out here.'"

To be sure, Monterey's days as the Sardine Capital of the World are long gone, yet California's first capital city has come of age in a new and exciting way. And, as I look around and see how picturesquely the new blends with the old (did you know that Monterey has more of its original adobe buildings than any other city in the state?), I can't help but think how the city's colorful history adds to its unique appeal. It is with this thought in mind that I can only hope that those who relive a part of Monterey's past through this work will remember its people—yes, the sardine fishermen and cannery workers among them—and credit them with the part they played in making this beautiful bayside community the warm and wonderful place it is today.

The Story in Pictures

Taken in the late 1800s, this picture shows the Pacific Coast Steamship Company pier, complete with its all-important freight and ticket office. In time this pier also became known as Fisherman's Wharf and Wharf Number One. The ships are unidentified, although personnel from the San Francisco Maritime Museum indicate that the vessel at anchor (center) might be a United States sea exploration ship. *Hathaway Collection*

A favorite of long-time Montereyans, this photo shows not only the 400-foot Pacific Coast Steamship Company pier (at a later date than the preceding picture; note the power pole, etc.) but also a trio of elegantly dressed ladies in their Victorian finery. *M. Oliver photo, Camera Masters Collection*

From Presidio Hill we get a different view of the Pacific Coast Steamship Company pier. The cannon in the foreground serves as a graphic reminder that El Castillo, Spain and Mexico's "fort on the hill," once occupied this site and protected California's capital city from intruders. The vessel at the wharf's end is thought to be the Pacific Coast Steamship Company's coastal freighter *Gipsy*, which was wrecked on Monterey's Macabee Beach (Cannery Row) on September 27, 1905. The pier to the right of the steamship company wharf is the Monterey and Salinas Valley Railroad Company pier (Depot Wharf). In the distance (left) is the bathhouse pier of the famed Hotel Del Monte. A portion of the hotel can be seen nestled in the trees above the bathhouse pier buildings. *C. Johnson photo, Hathaway Collection*

This photo shows the Pacific Coast Steamship Company pier as it appeared in 1900. Assorted buildings, including packing sheds, warehouses, and a least one fish market, can be seen. *M. Oliver photo, Hathaway Collection*

With Monterey's main wharf continuing to evolve, we see two recently completed warehouses. Old-timers state the structure to the right was operated by F. E. Booth's canning company. The steamship company building is visible in the background. *Monterey Public Library Collection*

Looking at the Booth Company warehouse from the seaward side, we can also see boats of the salmon variety as long-ago fishermen prepare to go to sea. *J. Oliver photo, Monterey Public Library Collection*

Monterey's early salmon fishing fleet presents a peaceful picture as the small boats dot the waters of Monterey Bay. *Hathaway Collection*

An assorted group of pioneer fishermen humorously display their catch of squid. The photo was taken near the end of Fisherman's Wharf and is thought to date back to the early 1920s. *Monterey Public Library Collection*

With development continuing to take place, things were seldom quiet on Wharf Number One. The steamship company vessel in the background is unidentified. The sign on the warehouse (center) reads:

MATTEO NAPOLI
WHOLESALE—RETAIL
ALL KINDS OF FISH
SHIPMENTS TO ALL PARTS OF THE STATE

L. Josselyn photo, Hathaway Collection

Whether they be called herring, pilchards, or sardines, there were plenty of fish in Monterey Bay around the turn of the century. This 1902 photo also shows the historic Custom House (left) and a new look to the entrance of Wharf Number One, as the recently completed Monterey Boating Club building dominates the scene. *M. Oliver photo, Monterey Public Library Collection*

Taken at a later date than the preceding picture, this photo proves that, in addition to fish, the Monterey of the early 1900s also boasted an elegant array of "dandily" dressed people. Unfortunately, the nature of the festive occasion is unrecorded. *Monterey Savings & Loan History Collection*

This photo give us a closer look at the Monterey Boating Club building as it appeared during the Great White Fleet's visit of 1908 as the fleet was on its way around the world. It was from the boating club's finger pier that visitors boarded launches for a once-in-a-lifetime visit to Uncle Sam's mighty white armada. The Great White Fleet went on to become the first battle fleet to circumnavigate the globe. *Colton Hall Collection*

Opposite the Monterey Boating Club building, and facing Monterey's main wharf, is the Custom House. Dating back to the 1820s, the Custom House is described as the oldest government building west of the Rockies. The structure's large walled-in yard was one of many nearby locations where fishermen stretched, dried, and mended their nets. In the background (left) a portion of old Monterey's popular Mission Art and Curio Store can be seen. *L. Josselyn photo, Hathaway Collection*

Only a stone's throw from the Custom House was the Booth Cannery. The main building shown here was destroyed by fire in 1903. Also visible are several stylish Montereyans—perhaps on a Sunday outing—and an assortment of net drying racks. *Monterey Public Library Collection*

33

As shown in this photo of 1928 (long after the Booth Cannery was rebuilt), the mending of nets often took place in a large field in front of the cannery. In the inset we get another view of the rebuilt Booth Cannery complex, circa 1930. *L. Josselyn photo, Hathaway Collection; inset, H. Waugh photo, Colton Hall Collection*

The crew members of the lampara boat *Thad* (with its accompanying lighter, or tow boat) are shown alongside the Booth Cannery pier as they are about to unload a catch of sardines. A portion of the Monterey wharf can be seen in the background. *T. Souza Collection*

The Booth Cannery pier presents a different picture when looking toward shore. Taken in 1938, this photo also shows the *Olympic* (one of Monterey's early purse seiners) as a morning fog obscures the background. *McKay photo & Collection*

In this view we see the Booth Cannery complex as it appeared from Fisherman's Wharf. In the foreground is the lampara boat *Caterina*, and to the right are three fishermen at work in a lighter. *Hathaway Collection*

35

36

The series of pictures on these two pages illustrate the process of unloading a heavily loaded lighter. Riding low in the water, her hold filled with sardines, the lighter *S. Oyama* is secured to the Booth Cannery pier. *Hathaway Collection*

A rare picture of a Pacific Coast Steamship Company vessel alongside its Monterey facility, this photo is thought to have been taken around 1910. A portion of the Booth Cannery pier can be seen to the far right. *F. Swain photo, Monterey Public Library Collection*

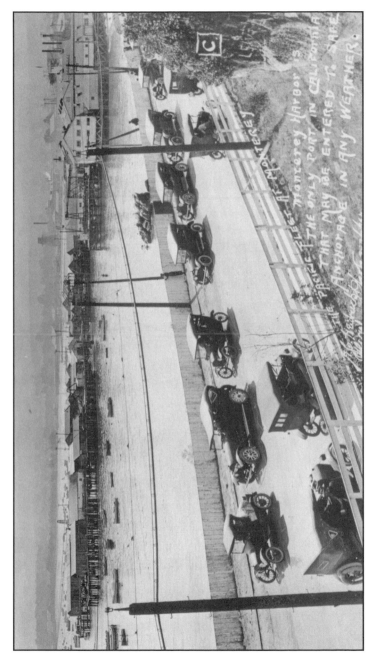

Here we see Fisherman's Wharf and a portion of the Booth Cannery (not to mention a parade of vintage automobiles) as they appeared from Presidio Curve during the Pacific Fleet's visit to Monterey Bay in August of 1919. A. Heidrick photo, Monterey Public Library Collection

39

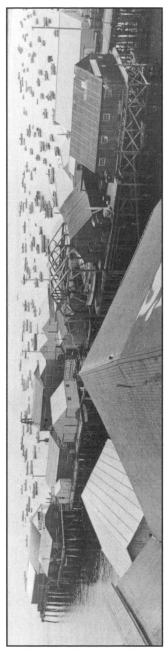

The Pacific Coast Steamship Company pier was eventually transformed into an all-purpose wharf. While this evolution transpired over a period of many years, no one can deny that it was impressive. The two pictures above are parts of a single panoramic photo that was taken from the roof of the Booth Cannery. The photo shows Fisherman's Wharf, and a portion of the fleet, long before Monterey's Municipal Wharf Number Two was built. *A. Heidrick photo, Monterey Public Library Collection*

In July, 1926, the coastal freighters *Cleone* (left) and *Daisy Freeman* were moored at the freighter facilities of Wharf Number One. *Hathaway Collection*

41

Taken in 1912, this rare photo shows portions of two Monterey wharves. To the left an Associated Oil Company tanker is moored to the Coalinga Oil and Transportation Company wharf (see below and next page for additional photos and information). To the right is the Monterey and Salinas Valley Railroad Company's "Depot Wharf" (reinforced with narrow-gauge rails). Originally built in 1874, and measuring 1,300 feet in length, the pier had shrunk considerably by 1912. *L. Slevin photo, Monterey County Library Collection*

Completed in 1904, the Coalinga Oil and Transportation Company wharf was built in the same general area as today's Monterey breakwater. The vessel to the right of the tugboat (center of picture) is the converted oil barge *Roderick Dhu.* Known as "The Masterpiece of 1873" (the year she was built), the *Roderick Dhu* set several international speed records. She met her end on Pacific Grove's Asilomar Beach in 1909. Behind the *Roderick Dhu* (and difficult to see) is the four-masted ship *Marion Chilcot.* The vessel at the far end of the pier is unidentified. *Colton Hall Collection*

In this later view of the Coalinga Oil and Transportation Company wharf (note power pole), a coastal freighter is seen at the left, with the masts of a much larger vessel visible on the opposite side. The pier was 650 feet long and contained 200,000 feet of lumber (exclusive of piles). The impressive structure was destroyed in Monterey's oil tank fire of 1924. *J. Oliver photo, Monterey Public Library Collection*

43

The construction of Monterey's much-needed Municipal Wharf Number Two got its start in 1925. *Monterey Public Library Collection*

By May of 1926 the size and shape of Monterey's 1,750-foot Wharf Number Two was apparent to all. *Monterey Public Library Collection*

Upon its completion Wharf Number Two—which boasted a 50- by 310-foot fire-proof warehouse at its seaward end—became a busy place. In this photo a coastal freighter is moored alongside the warehouse building, with the masts of a second such ship visible above its roof (see inset). *Hathaway Collection*

A "modern" tractor-trailer rig boasting a load of Hovden's Portola Brand sardines is prominent in this view of Wharf Number Two. A portion of the coastal freighter *Crescent City* (left) can also be seen in this early 1927 photo. The *Crescent City* was a regular on the San Francisco to Monterey run. On July 27 of that year, while making her way to Monterey in a dense coastal fog, she was wrecked on the bay's north shore (approximately four miles from the Santa Cruz lighthouse). *A. Heidrick photo, Monterey Public Library Collection*

Allen Knight Maritime Museum Collection

On March 17, 1928, the largest ship ever to have docked at Monterey's Wharf Number Two up to that time arrived on the scene. With a cargo of 872 tons of tin plate for the American Can Company (located near Cannery Row), the 10,000-ton freighter *Robin Goodfellow* dwarfed the new wharf. *Allen Knight Maritime Museum Collection*

46

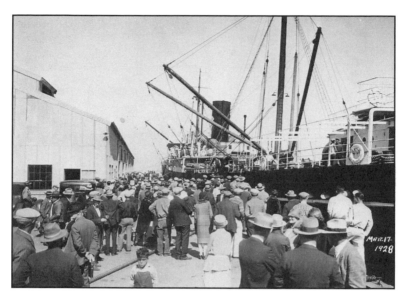

With her docking and unloading operations witnessed by hundreds of locals, the *Robin Goodfellow* proved that Wharf Number Two was capable of handling large, oceangoing freighters. *Monterey Public Library Collection*

This photo gives us a closer look at the unloading operations of the *Robin Goodfellow*. *Monterey Public Library Collection*

This 1928 photo shows Wharf Number Two in the background (could that be the *Robin Goodfellow* on the far side of the warehouse?). To the left is the original Monterey Boating Club building, which had become the popular Pop Ernest restaurant. Pop Ernest is well remembered on the Monterey Peninsula and is known as the man who originated and perfected the abalone steak. The platform in the foreground is part of Ferrante's Landing (discussed in the next caption). *L. Josselyn photo, Hathaway Collection*

Looking toward the Custom House from Pop Ernest's restaurant, we see skids used for hauling boats from the water prior to repair (right). Ferrante's Landing is to the left. It was built in the early 1900s by Peter Ferrante in conjunction with the Booth Company. Early on the landing was especially popular with lampara-boat fishermen. It was used for such things as the storage of skiffs and the mending and drying of nets before being torn down in 1938. *Hathaway Collection*

As indicated earlier, the original Monterey Boating Club building (at the entrance of Wharf Number One) became the home of the popular Pop Ernest restaurant. This photo, taken from the Custom House gardens, shows the building—complete with a rear addition—as it took on a "touristy" look. The building was destroyed by fire in 1975. *D. Mineo Collection*

49

Taken in the late 1920s, this photo shows Fisherman's Wharf as seen from the west side (opposite the Pop Ernest building). A portion of the Booth Cannery is visible to the left. *L. Josselyn photo, Hathaway Collection*

Later in years than the preceding photo, and taken from a similar vantage point, this image shows considerable changes to Fisherman's Wharf. The aging Booth Cannery is to the left. *Monterey Public Library Collection*

51

G. Seideneck photo, Hathaway Collection

Similar views, photographed at different times from slightly different locations, show the west side of Fisherman's Wharf. The Critchlow boat hoist, machine shop (to its right), and repair area are prominent in both pictures. No date is given for the top photo, while 1947 is listed as the year the bottom picture was taken.
F. Harbick photo, Hathaway Collection

Rounded tanks, rusted stacks, weathered pilings, and waiting skiffs add a nostalgic touch to this view of the west side of Wharf Number One. The tank in the foreground (left) was a hot-water tank. The water was used for a variety of purposes, including the tanning of nets and the cooking of anchovies. *G. Seideneck photo, Hathaway Collection*

This 1947 photo shows the west side of Fisherman's Wharf from a seldom seen angle (looking toward shore). The Harbor House complex is at the far end. *F. Harbick photo, Hathaway Collection*

The lampara boat *Pleasure* is in the foreground in this early view of the east side of Fisherman's Wharf (looking toward shore). *Hathaway Collection*

Taken at a later date than the preceding photo, this picture gives us a more complete view of Wharf Number One's east side. *Hathaway Collection*

Except for minor changes, a few signs, and a little paint, this scene is remarkably similar to those on the opposite page. G. *Seideneck photo, Hathaway Collection*

Skiffs of various shapes and sizes cluster around a loading ramp on Wharf Number One. F. *Harbick photo, Hathaway Collection*

Celebrating the end of a successful 1937 season, local boat owners and fishermen put on a never-to-be-forgotten feed for the people of Monterey on Wharf Number Two. The tab for the great event came to $13,000. *R. Ruppel photo, Monterey Peninsula Herald Collection*

W. Morgan photo, Hathaway Collection

The blessing of the fleet—a part of Monterey's traditional Santa Rosalia Festival—
is an important event on the Monterey Peninsula that originally took place "at the
time of the full moon" in the month of September. These pictures of the blessing
of the fleet ceremonies were taken in different years, by different photographers,
with the vantage point in both cases having been Wharf Number Two (looking in
opposite directions). *L. Blaisdell photo, Monterey Public Library Collection*

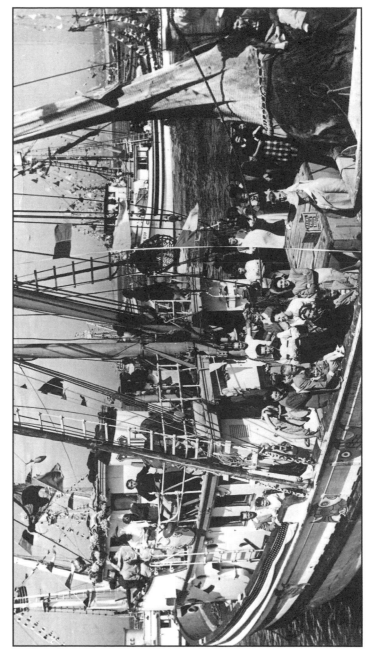

Along with parades, feasts, and other functions, the Santa Rosalia festivals featured Monterey's fishing fleet. The purse seiner *U.S. Liberator* is the vessel pictured here. *L. Blaisdell photo, Monterey Public Library Collection*

R. Blaisdell photo & Collection

As the crowds from the festivals and the blessing of the fleet ceremonies dwindled, the fishermen of old Monterey gathered in quiet corners of Fisherman's Wharf. It was here that they played cards, enjoyed the sunshine, and talked about fishing and their experiences at sea. *W. Morgan photo, J. Stracuzzi Collection*

As the years rolled on and good friends departed, the gatherings grew smaller and the memories began to fade. *W. Morgan photo, J. Stracuzzi Collection*

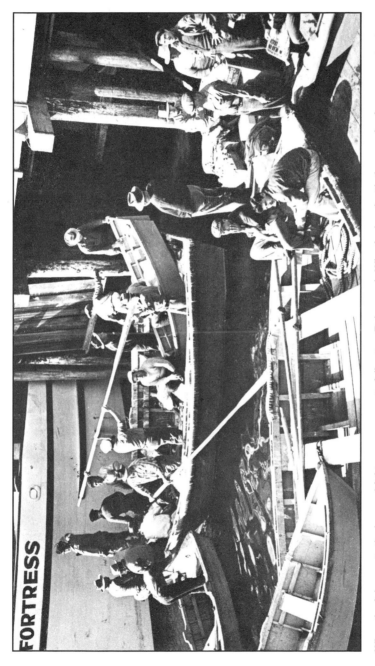

When the fish were in the bay and fishing season was in full swing, Fisherman's Wharf echoed with the sounds of men preparing to go to sea. *R. Ruppel photo, D. Mineo Collection*

Everything needed to be ready before a sardine boat set out, as once the fish were spotted there was no time to spare. The men shown here are inspecting a brail net and hoop used to lift fish from the hold of a vessel and transport them to a hopper. Hoppers were floating containers anchored near the canneries. The fish were pumped from the hoppers to the canneries, where they were processed. *G. Seideneck photo, Hathaway Collection*

After a busy night of fishing, the morning after often found an exhausted crew repairing nets and preparing for another trip to sea. The tanning tanks of Wharf Number One are seen in the background. (For a brief explanation of the tanning process, see page 64.) *Hathaway Collection*

Here we see the half-ring boat *Santa Maria* at the tanning tanks of Wharf Number One. *Hathaway Collection*

Without strong nets the sardine industry would not have been the success that it was. To help preserve the nets, fishermen periodically subjected them to a tanning process that strengthened the cotton fibers (of which the early nets were made) and greatly enhanced their life span. The tannic solution was obtained from the bark of oak trees. In later years the nets were tarred instead of tanned. Here and on the facing page we see purse seiner nets being dipped into tanning tanks on Wharf Number One. *R. Ruppel photo, D. Mineo Collection*

R. Ruppel photo, D. Mineo Collection

65

When nets became damaged, they were often loaded aboard trucks and taken to nearby fields, yards, or streets, where they were stretched, inspected, and repaired. Here we see a net being loaded aboard a truck on Wharf Number Two. *F. Harbick photo, Hathaway Collection*

As suggested in the preceding caption, the mending of nets took place wherever a spot big enough could be found. These two photos show crew members making themselves comfortable as they go about the task of repairing their nets. *Hathaway Collection*

G. Seideneck photo, Hathaway Collection

G. Seideneck photo, Hathaway Collection

68

G. Seideneck photo, Hathaway Collection

As the series of pictures on these two pages illustrate, there is an art to "stacking" a purse seiner net, and it takes various members of the crew working together to do the job right. A closer look at the photos also reveals floats of various shapes, sizes, and kinds, as well as the stern section/turntable of a purse seiner, where the nets are kept. *G. Seideneck photo, Hathaway Collection*

R. Reinstedt photo & Collection

R. Reinstedt photo & Collection

Although Monterey's heyday as a fishing port came to an end in the 1950s, scenes similar to those shown in the photos on these two pages—taken circa 1977 on Wharf Number Two—could still be seen many years later. *R. Reinstedt photo & Collection*

This photo takes us back to the mid-1930s. It is a favorite among old-timers and shows the members of a purse seiner crew as they head for their vessel and a night of fishing. *F. Harpick photo, Hathaway Collection*

Purse seiner crews head for their boats and what they hope will be a profitable night's catch (late 1930s). *F. Harbick photo, Hathaway Collection*

Thought to have been taken in the early 1940s, this photo shows a motor-powered skiff and a harbor full of fishing vessels. *G. Seideneck photo, Hathaway Collection*

R. Ruppel photo, Allen Knight Maritime Museum Collection

Once the fishermen reached their boats, the hunt began. Purse seiners *John R.* and *Lina V.* are pictured here. *R. Ruppel photo, Hathaway Collection*

When the sardines were spotted, it was "All hands on deck!" In this view the fish have been encircled and the brailing process (lifting the fish from the water) has begun. The man in the skiff had many duties, one of them being to keep an eye on the net and prevent it from closing. *R. Ruppel photo, Hathaway Collection*

This photo provides a closer look at the duties of the man in the skiff. With an oar in his hands (usually a long pole was used), he was able to keep the skiff from drifting too close to the vessel. This kept the net open and enabled the brailing process to continue. *Hathaway Collection*

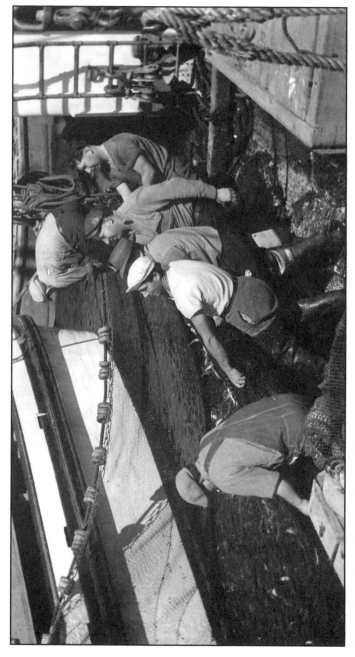

On occasion, when a boat caught more fish than it could haul or had reached its limit, the skipper would call in a second vessel and share the catch. In this scene crew members of the purse seiner *City of Monterey* (foreground) keep the net taut as men from the *California Rose* prepare to brail the fish. *Hathaway Collection*

Here we have a graphic illustration of brailing. Old-timers describe a brail of this type as "the horn of plenty." After the fish were lifted from the sea, they were dumped into the hold of the ship. *Hathaway Collection*

When a load of sardines was caught and the nets were back aboard the boats, the purse seiners would head for the canneries, where the process of brailing the fish into the hoppers would begin. Cannery Row is at the far left in this photo, while at the far right crew members of the *Santa Rosa* prepare to brail the fish from the hold of their vessel into a hopper. *R. Ruppel photo, Hathaway Collection*

With Cannery Row as a backdrop, this scene shows that activity around the hoppers wasn't confined to purse seiners. Pictured here are boats and lighters of the squid variety as they wait their turn at the hoppers. *R. Ruppel photo, Hathaway Collection*

81

R. Ruppel photo, D. Mineo Collection

R. Ruppel photo, D. Mineo Collection

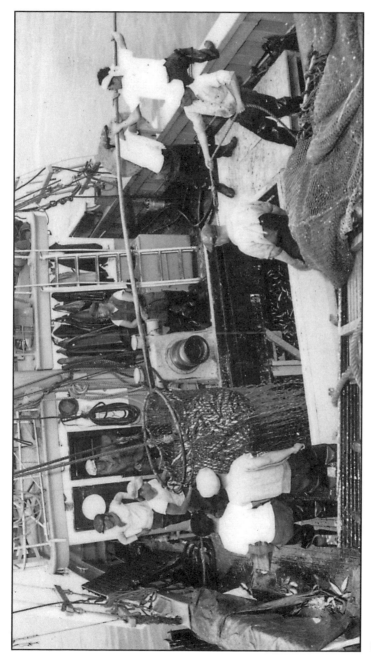

The process of brailing fish from the hold of a vessel is graphically illustrated in the photos on these two pages. *R. Ruppel photo, D. Mineo Collection*

Here and on the facing page we see the brailing of sardines from a heavily loaded purse seiner (note the quantity of fish on the deck). During exceptionally large catches like these, a big purse seiner would often bring in more than 150 tons of sardines. *R. Ruppel photo, D. Mineo Collection*

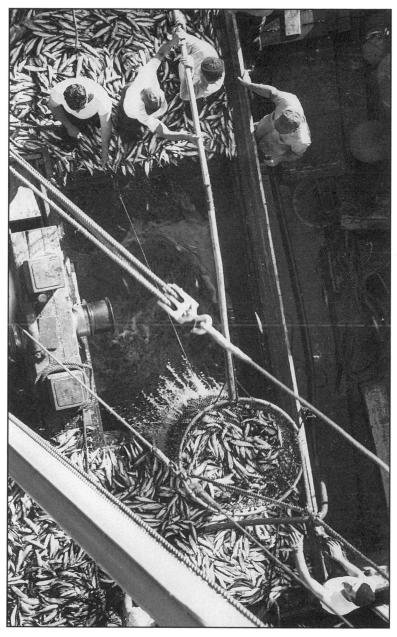

R. Ruppel photo, D. Mineo Collection

Tied to a buoy off Cannery Row, the purse seiner *California Rose* waits her turn at the hoppers, filled to capacity (and perhaps a bit more) with an estimated 160 tons of sardines. This 1936 photo shows how low in the water a purse seiner would ride when it was fully loaded with fish. *S. Bruno photo, V. Bruno Collection*

Alongside the hopper (a portion of which is visible in the foreground), the crew of the *California Rose* prepare to brail the fish from the hold of their ship. *S. Bruno photo, V. Bruno Collection*

With the crew of the *California Rose* intent on brailing, we see the vessel's deck awash with fish. A crew member at the time (1936) stated that the *California Rose* was capable of carrying 132 tons of fish in her hold and an additional 28 tons on her decks. *S. Bruno photo, V. Bruno Collection*

As illustrated in this aged postcard view, after the fish were brailed from the hold of a ship, they were dumped into hoppers (center). From there they were pumped via pipes to the nearby canneries. *Hathaway Collection*

87

In the mid-1930s thankful fishermen and delighted Montereyans welcomed the introduction of the short-wave radio to the fleet. While the men at sea exchanged information, people at home gathered around their marine-band short-wave radios and followed their progress. Here a proud Salvatore (Badazza) Russo (an early user of the short-wave radio) poses in the pilothouse of the purse seiner *Western Star. T. Russo Collection*

Not all of the action took place at sea—or concerned sardines—as we see in this picture taken from Wharf Number Two. The photo shows crew members of a lampara boat brailing squid from the hold of their vessel. The lampara boat *Santa Rosalia* is in the background. *Monterey Peninsula Herald Collection*

The brailing process continues as the squid are hoisted to a wholesale outlet on Wharf Number Two. *Monterey Peninsula Herald Collection*

After a long and tiring trip, no one looked forward to the job of climbing into the hold of a vessel to help with the brailing. *Monterey Peninsula Herald Collection*

Fishing for sardines was most often done at night, when the phosphorescent glow of the fish could best be seen. Here and on the next six pages are a series of pictures taken at night that show the process of "bringing in the fish." After the nets were set before the oncoming fish and the sardines were "pursed," the process of drawing in the nets began. *T. Russo Collection*

As the purse draws tighter, the sea becomes alive with fish. *T. Russo Collection*

93

The brailing process begins. *T. Russo Collection*

With quick reactions and a sturdy pole, the man in the skiff is able to keep his craft away from the ship, enabling the brailing process to continue. *T. Russo Collection*

A few of the sardines were able to flee the confines of the net, but unless the net was damaged, or a mistake was made, the few that got away were not worth counting. *T. Russo Collection*

Brailing took considerable skill and a lot of hard work. *T. Russo Collection*

From the sea to the hold was a one-way trip for the sardine. *G. Robinson photo, Hathaway Collection*

After the fish were unloaded and the purse seiners were moored, it was back to the wharf for Monterey's men of the sea. *G. Seideneck photo, Hathaway Collection*

While the fleet rests and waits for another night of fishing, a lone crew member returns to Wharf Number One, perhaps after doing maintenance work aboard his vessel. *G. Seideneck photo, Hathaway Collection*

From Wharf Number Two we get a partial view of Monterey's early fleet. Fisherman's Wharf and a few canneries can be seen in the distance. *L. Blaisdell photo, Colton Hall Collection*

Vessels of various shapes and sizes, including lampara boats, salmon boats, pleasure craft, hook and liners, and lighters, are visible in this 1928 photo. Wharf Number One is to the right. The large building on the left is the Hotel San Carlos, which operated from 1925 to 1983. *L. Josselyn photo, Hathaway Collection*

From a different vantage point we get another view of the Monterey shoreline, circa late 1920s. The Hotel San Carlos is on the left, with the vessel in the foreground being identified as either a Fish and Game boat or a research ship. *L. Josselyn photo, Hathaway Collection*

Among the mainstays of Monterey's early fishing fleet were the lampara boats, a few of which are pictured here along with their skiffs. *Hathaway Collection*

L. Blaisdell photo, Monterey Public Library Collection

The harbor scenes changed with the years. In these photos we see a peaceful Monterey harbor boasting several vessels of the purse seiner variety. *L. Blaisdell photo, Monterey Public Library Collection*

When Monterey was called "The Sardine Capital of the World," her harbor was filled with purse seiners of all descriptions. Other than a sky of masts and a crowded harbor, of interest here are the carefully covered nets on the sterns of the boats. The nets were covered to help protect and preserve them. *G. Seideneck photo, Hathaway Collection*

The Monterey of the late 1930s and early 1940s was a place of proud vessels and a picturesque harbor. *R. Ruppel photo, Hathaway Collection*

As time passed, a marine service station was added to the seaward end of Wharf Number One's tanning tank pier. In this photo the purse seiner *Cerrito Bros.* is about to take on fuel. *F. Harbick photo, Hathaway Collection*

A second view of the tanning tank pier's marine service station also shows the bow of the flag-bedecked purse seiner *Camarello*. G. Seideneck photo, Hathaway Collection

At the end of Wharf Number One's second finger pier was a second marine service station. The *Thelma Kay* is tied to the pier in this 1947 photo. *Allen Knight Maritime Museum Collection*

Also tied to the wharf's second finger pier is the half-ring boat *Geraldine-Ann*. Happy crew members pose for their picture atop the pilothouse as an overflow catch fills the deck. *Allen Knight Maritime Museum Collection*

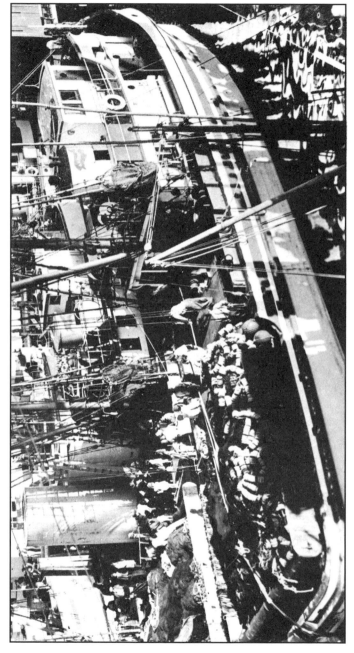

This busy scene took place near the end of Fisherman's Wharf (looking toward the finger piers shown in previous photos). Said to have been taken during a Santa Rosalia Festival, the picture not only illustrates the size of a large purse seiner but also shows a group of Montereyans about to board the vessel. *R. Ruppel photo, Hathaway Collection*

110

The purse seiner *Petrina F.* adds to the atmosphere of Wharf Number One. *Hathaway Collection*

The warehouse at the end of Wharf Number Two serves as a backdrop for this photo of the purse seiner *Belvedere,* taken in 1939. *Allen Knight Maritime Museum Collection*

Taken in May, 1952, this photo shows the half-ring boat *Nyna Rose.* The purse seiner in the background is unidentified. *Allen Knight Maritime Museum Collection*

Even though she was originally built for sardines, the *St. Mary* was eventually converted to a drag boat (a vessel that drags the bottom for its catch). *N. Vingrad photo, Hathaway Collection*

The purse seiner *El Padre* in 1937. *Allen Knight Maritime Museum Collection*

The purse seiner *Endeavor* in 1948. *Allen Knight Maritime Museum Collection*

The purse seiner *City of Monterey,* December 24, 1937. *Allen Knight Maritime Museum Collection*

The purse seiner *Star of Monterey.* Inset shows her heavily loaded and riding low in the water next to a Cannery Row hopper. *Monterey Peninsula Herald Collection; inset, Hathaway Collection*

Monterey's purse seiners came in varying sizes, but as shown in a number of the photos in this book, they had the same basic design. The trim lines of these vessels were admired by people from throughout the world.

115

What would a fishing port be without seagulls? In this scene the purse seiner *Sea Giant* is making its way into the Monterey harbor after unloading its catch at one of the nearby hoppers. As the crew cleaned the boat and threw overboard the sardines that were found on the deck, the ever-present seagulls followed in the craft's wake and fought over every morsel. *Allen Knight Maritime Museum Collection*

The *Diana* was one of Monterey's best-known purse seiners. She also boasted one of the fleet's best records. After the sardines disappeared, the *Diana*, like most of the large purse seiners, headed south and called southern California's waters home. She eventually returned to Monterey, where for many years she was the only pre-World War II purse seiner in the harbor. The photo inset shows part of the *Diana*'s stern. It was taken in Monterey forty years after the full view was taken. *Allen Knight Maritime Museum Collection; inset, R. Reinstedt photo & Collection*

R. Reinstedt photo & Collection

R. Reinstedt photo & Collection

118

R. Reinstedt photo & Collection

Although many years have passed since Monterey was The Sardine Capital of the World, it still boasts many boats with colorful pasts. To walk among them and listen to their sounds, and the sounds of the fishermen as they prepare to go to sea, is to recapture a bit of the romance, the mystique, and the personalities of the men and their vessels. The pictures on these two pages were taken in the Monterey marina long after the sardine was king. *R. Reinstedt photo & Collection*

119

The Monterey marina, officially known as the Monterey Municipal Marina, was completed in 1960. Shown here circa 1979, and on the facing page circa 1981, it was reconstructed in 1996. Thanks to its popularity with owners of both pleasure and commercial craft, there is often a waiting list for an empty berth. *City of Monterey Collection*

Monterey Public Library Collection

With the completion of the breakwater (1934) and the marina (1960), the Monterey harbor became a much safer haven for vessels of varying shapes, sizes, and uses. This, however, didn't stop old-timers from talking about the many storms that brought havoc to the Monterey harbor (with the storms of 1915, 1919, 1943, and 1953 being among the most memorable). The photos shown here illustrate the aftermath of the April 29, 1915, storm, in which more than fifty vessels were blown upon the beach. *Monterey Public Library Collection*

122

According to aged accounts, ninety-three vessels were strewn along the shore during the November 26, 1919, storm. *Monterey Public Library Collection*

Forty boats were beached by the December 8, 1943, storm. This photo was taken from Wharf Number Two. *Monterey Public Library Collection*

Among the vessels blown ashore during the storm of February 23, 1953, were the purse seiners *New Hope* and *Cerrito Bros*. Here, a lone Montereyan braves the breakers as he attempts to pull away from the grounded ships. *L. Blasidell photo, Monterey Public Library Collection*

As the tide receded, the *New Hope* and the *Cerrito Bros.* were left high and dry on the Monterey beach. Both vessels were eventually salvaged. *R. Reinstedt photo & Collection*

In addition to storms, fog, wind, rocky coastlines, treacherous currents, and unpredictable weather, boat owners and fishermen also had to be concerned with fire. This photo shows the lampara boat *Crivello No. 1* burning in the Monterey harbor. *Allen Knight Maritime Museum Collection*

Long before the demise of the sardine and the coming of convention facilities changed her ways, Monterey was a busy fishing community with a charm all its own. This photo, taken from the Hotel San Carlos in the late 1920s, gives us a glimpse of the town and its waterfront, with the battleship *New Mexico* in the background. *Monterey Public Library Collection*

In rounding Monterey's waterfront and heading toward Cannery Row, picturesque vistas of the wharves and the Booth Cannery complex were to be had. This view is from Presidio Hill, July 13, 1928. *L. Josselyn photo, Hathaway Collection*

126

This view of the Monterey harbor and Wharf Number Two as seen from Presidio Curve (closer to Cannery Row) offers a snowcapped Mt. Toro as a backdrop. *D. Eaton Collection*

An aerial view of Wharf Number One and the Booth Cannery complex (left of the wharf) as they appeared on August 9, 1937, may help to bring many of the previous pictures into perspective. Wharf Number One (Fisherman's Wharf) shows little resemblance to the original Pacific Coast Steamship Company pier as seen on pages 24 and 25. *McKay photo & Collection*

Here we see Wharf Number One and the elaborate Booth Cannery complex as viewed from the air in March, 1938. *McKay photo & Collection*

Closer to Cannery Row (with the San Carlos and E. B. Gross Cannery complexes visible in the lower right corner), this photo shows the Monterey breakwater, the Booth Cannery, and Monterey's wharves Number One and Number Two. *McKay photo & Collection*

In this aerial view of the south end of Cannery Row, we get a closer look at the San Carlos Cannery (closest to the breakwater) and the E. B. Gross Company. This picture and the one on the opposite page were both taken in 1938. *McKay photo & Collection*

This early view of the E. B. Gross Canning Company (established 1919) was taken from the corner of Reeside Avenue and Cannery Row. *R. Reinstedt Collection*

C. Tuttle photo, Hathaway Collection

The Associated Oil Company's "tank farm" was located between Presidio Hill and the San Carlos and E. B. Gross canning complexes (near the current Monterey breakwater). The tanks fed oil to the tankers that called at Monterey. On September 14, 1924, the tanks were struck by lightning, resulting in a fire that threatened the entire Monterey waterfront and destroyed the oil company pier. *R. Reinstedt Postcard Collection*

Soldiers from the Monterey Presidio were used to help fight the 1924 fire, with two losing their lives to the inferno. Aged accounts describe the blaze as "the greatest conflagration in the history of Monterey and one of the greatest oil fires of California." *L. Josselyn photo, Hathaway Collection*

C. Tuttle photo, Hathaway Collection

As seen from different vantage points, billowing clouds of smoke from the oil tank fire continued to darken the sky, creating considerable concern for people of the Peninsula as well as for those in outlying areas. In the bottom photo the magnificent Murray Mansion of old Cannery Row is visible in the foreground. *Hathaway Collection*

The Murray Mansion (shown above and on the preceding page) was built by Hugh Tevis (son of Lloyd Tevis, a name familiar to California history buffs) in 1901. In 1904 James A. Murray, a Montana mining millionaire, purchased the property (thus the name most locals know it by). Although Murray died in 1921, the estate remained a showplace along the Monterey waterfront for many years. In 1944 the buildings were demolished. Canneries and reduction plants soon followed. Today the beautiful Monterey Plaza Hotel & Spa (a portion of which is shown to the left) occupies the site. *R. Reinstedt Postcard Collection (circa 1907)*

R. Reinstedt photo & Collection

136

Situated north of the Murray Mansion (near the center of today's Cannery Row), the Pacific Fish Company (circa 1908) is said to have been one of the earliest major canning operations on the Monterey coast. *Monterey Public Library Collection*

Parts of Cannery Row and the United States Pacific Fleet are seen from the roof of the Monterey Canning Company warehouse in August, 1919. A. *Heidrick photo, Monterey Public Library Collection*

This photo shows the unloading pier of the Hovden Company cannery. The picture was taken when the fish were unloaded by cable, before hoppers came into use. The pier was located at the north end of Cannery Row (where the Monterey Bay Aquarium is now located) and was one of the first to be built. *T. Souza Collection*

A second cannery pier can be seen in this photo, along with a variety of early vessels. *L. Josselyn photo, Hathaway Collection*

Here we see a rare view of Cannery Row's canneries and their picturesque piers from the sea. The structures in the foreground are thought to be part of the Carmel Canning Company complex. With the buildings made of wood and saturated with fish oil, it is not difficult to imagine the destruction that could be caused by the spark from a careless match—or, in later years, from an arsonist's torch. *Hathaway Collection*

Long after the picture on the facing page was taken, and as Cannery Row "went modern," fish by the thousands were piped into the canneries from nearby hoppers. Shown here are fish being disgorged from a hopper pipe, where they continued their trip—via a fish elevator—to the weighing platform and cutting tables. *G. Robinson photo, Hathaway Collection*

141

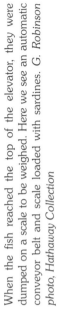

When the fish reached the top of the elevator, they were dumped on a scale to be weighed. Here we see an automatic conveyor belt and scale loaded with sardines. *G. Robinson photo, Hathaway Collection*

In this second view of a fish elevator, we can readily see how the fish were brought into the canneries, with the water being left behind. *J. Stracuzzi Collection*

142

As shown in this postcard photo (said to have been taken in the mid teens), in the early days people of all ages were hired to work in the canneries. At this time the heads and tails of the fish were cut by hand. *M. Rieder, Publ., Los Angeles, California*

As time marched on, the heads and tails of the fish were removed by machines instead of by hand. Here the fish are being loaded into a cutting machine. *G. Robinson photo, Hathaway Collection*

144

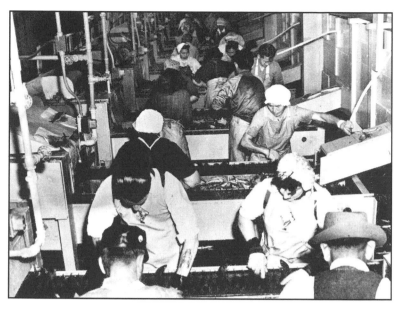

This photo gives us a view of another kind of cutting machine (referred to as a double cutter). *R. Ruppel photo, D. Mineo Collection*

At the packing table (also referred to as the canning table), workers packed the headless and tailless fish into cans. *R. Ruppel photo, D. Mineo Collection*

A second packing table scene shows a group of "Monterey's finest" as they busily fill oval cans with tasty sardines. *F. Harbick photo, Hathaway Collection*

Unique to this packing-table photo are the tall, round (one-pound) cans the fish are being packed into, as opposed to the flat, oval containers that had become a trademark of the Monterey sardine industry. *Hathaway Collection*

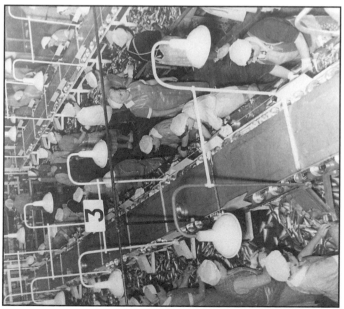

Packing tables came in a variety of shapes and sizes, and the women who worked them put in long hours. *G. Robinson photo, Hathaway Collection*

147

At the packing table (canning line) each can was salted (see funnel-shaped salter in the foreground). From the packing table the cans headed for the steam cookers. *F. Harbick photo, Hathaway Collection*

From the steam cookers, where the fish received the first of two cooking processes, the cans went through draining machines, as pictured here. The machine to the left was for the tall, round cans, while the machine in the center was used for the oval cans. The drainers would turn the cans upside down, enabling the excess water, fish oil, etc., to drain out. After the drainers the cans received their final ingredients (such as tomato sauce, mustard, and olive oil) and were sent to the sealing machines. *T. Souza Collection*

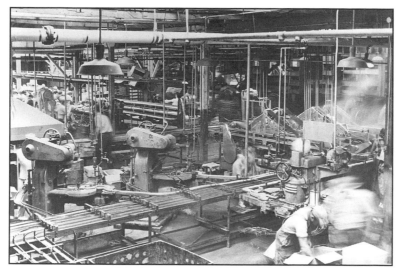

Portions of the old canneries were mazes of machinery. In this view the Hovden plant's sealing machines (which sealed the lids on the cans) are seen in the foreground. *Monterey Public Library Collection*

After being sealed, the cans were cleaned and placed in large iron containers (baskets). The containers were than wheeled into the cooking chambers (retorts). *R. Ruppel photo, Hathaway Collection*

A retort operator adjusts his gauges as the canned sardines are cooked under pressure. With this being the last phase of the canning process, the fish were then taken to the warehouses, where they were labeled and stored. *G. Robinson photo, Hathaway Collection*

When the Row was "alive" and the fish were being canned in back-to-back shifts, freight trains brought countless boxcars to the warehouse sidings to be filled with sardines destined for locations throughout the nation. *T. Souza Collection*

A view of Cannery Row from the air shows the railroad line and some of its sidings. The northernmost portion of Cannery Row is also shown in this 1937 picture. *McKay photo & Collection*

151

The northern half of Cannery Row can be seen in this photo. Also visible are parts of New Monterey and Pacific Grove, along with China Point (Point Cabrillo), Lover's Point, and Point Pinos (in the distance). The picture was taken in 1938. *McKay photo & Collection*

The elaborate Del Mar Canning Company cannery and warehouse complex is at the center of each of these photos of northern Cannery Row. *McKay photo & Collection*

153

Cannery Row of the late 1930s was perhaps the busiest, noisiest, most colorful, and most profitable street on the Monterey Peninsula. It was also the smelliest! The Row's distinctive overhead walkways were mainly used to transport the fish from the canneries to the warehouses. *G. Seideneck photo, Hathaway Collection*

The Hovden Cannery complex dominated the northern end of Cannery Row. Canning the famed Portola brand sardines, the plant was one of the first to open, and the last to close. *Hathaway Collection*

When no sardines could be found in or around Monterey Bay, the fleet headed south. Amid hopes and prayers of better things to come, the Row was kept alive with sardines that were trucked in from more plentiful fishing grounds off the southern California coast. *F. Harbick photo, Hathaway Collection*

Looking south from the vicinity of the Hovden complex, we see a dying Cannery Row. Wing Chong's grocery store (made famous by John Steinbeck's 1945 novel *Cannery Row*) can be seen at the right. Also on the right the Cypress Cafe proudly advertises "Tables for Ladies." *F. Harbick photo, Hathaway Collection*

This photo was taken slightly south of the Hovden Cannery and directly opposite the Marine Biological Laboratory of Ed "Doc" Ricketts (again of Steinbeck fame). The truck is loaded with such Cannery Row hardware as fish trays and fish cooling containers (baskets). To the right is the original site of Flora's Lone Star "house of pleasure," which was well known locally long before Steinbeck immortalized the establishment in *Cannery Row. T. Souza Collection*

Tucked between two larger buildings was the Marine Biological Laboratory—and home—of Ed Ricketts. Known to countless Steinbeck fans as "Doc," Ricketts was also a well-known and respected member of the Cannery Row community. In later years, "Doc's Lab" became a private men's club. It is now the property of the City of Monterey. *R. Reinstedt photo & Collection*

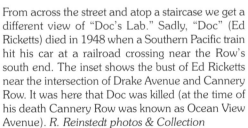

From across the street and atop a staircase we get a different view of "Doc's Lab." Sadly, "Doc" (Ed Ricketts) died in 1948 when a Southern Pacific train hit his car at a railroad crossing near the Row's south end. The inset shows the bust of Ed Ricketts near the intersection of Drake Avenue and Cannery Row. It was here that Doc was killed (at the time of his death Cannery Row was known as Ocean View Avenue). *R. Reinstedt photos & Collection*

A glimpse of Monterey Bay from the windows and back deck of "Doc's Lab" (circa 1978). *R. Reinstedt photos & Collection*

159

Merchants and landowners, together with Steinbeck fans and history buffs, continue to fear the fires that occasionally strike the aged and decaying buildings that still dot the Row. This scene shows the 1951 Westgate-Sun Harbor Cannery and warehouse fire. The Del Mar Canning Company was originally located at this site. *W. Morgan photo, Hathaway Collection*

This view from the tracks indicates why the Westgate-Sun Harbor complex (including the fish reduction plant on the left) was declared a total loss. Along with the buildings, $1,500,000 worth of fish went up in flames. *W. Morgan photo, Hathaway Collection*

In 1953 the Custom House Packing Company cannery was added to the list of structures destroyed by fire. *R. Ruppel photo, Hathaway Collection*

As seen from a neighboring building, firemen fought the Custom House Packing Company fire from various locations. Unfortunately, the 1950s-vintage firefighting equipment was no match for the flames. *W. Morgan photo, Hathaway Collection*

In 1956 the San Carlos Cannery at the Row's south end was lost in a dramatic night fire. *R. Blaisdell photo & Collection*

Seen here silhouetted against fire, water, and smoke, firemen did all in their power to keep the San Carlos Cannery fire from spreading. *R. Blaisdell photo & Collection*

The morning after leaves nothing to the imagination as a ghostly fishing fleet is seen through the charred remains of the San Carlos Cannery building. *R. Blaisdell photo & Collection*

Above we see part of the Row's back side from the Monterey breakwater. The San Carlos Cannery was located at the extreme left. *R. Blaisdell photo & Collection*

From the San Carlos Cannery shore we get a closer look at the weathered buildings of the once-prosperous Peninsula Packing Company. *R. Blaisdell photo & Collection*

166

From the sea we get a different view of several of the buildings shown on the facing page. The San Carlos Cannery was located on the flat at the left of the picture. Its warehouse survived the 1956 fire and can be seen on the opposite side of the street (see page 164 for a second view of the warehouse). Perhaps of more interest to fans of sea creatures is the killer-whale fin that is visible in the foreground. *L. Blaisdell photo & Collection*

An abundance of weathered wood, rotting pilings, rusted metal, and broken windows made it clear that portions of the Row had been long neglected and left to the elements. *R. Reinstedt photo & Collection*

Eyeless windows stare out to sea as old Cannery Row buildings survey the scene.
R. Reinstedt photo & Collection

Long ago, when the canneries were bustling and bursting with fish, many work-ers lived in nearby cottages. There they waited for the signal that would call them to work. Then, as blasts from cannery whistles announced that a new catch had arrived or a new shift was about to begin, the workers would drop what they were doing and head for the hustle and bustle of the Row. *R. Reinstedt photo & Collection*

170

With the echoes of the cannery whistles fading into the past, aged Cannery Row signs lost both their meaning and their legibility. *R. Reinstedt photo & Collection*

As the weeds grew and the metal rusted, the Row sat silent, waiting for a better time. *R. Blaisdell photo & Collection*

Neglected buildings survived on the Row to remind photographers, history buffs, and aged Montereyans of the hurly-burly of yesteryear. *R. Blaisdell photo & Collection*

Aged and unused artifacts of odd shapes and sizes were once common sights on and around Cannery Row. Today, however, scattered among a hodgepodge of buildings (both old and new) one finds interesting shops, inviting coffeehouses, gourmet restaurants, noisy night spots, seaside vistas, waterfront hotels, and, of course, the fabulous Monterey Bay Aquarium. Yes, the streets are once again bustling with people, but for the dwindling number of old-timers Cannery Row is mostly memories of a time that was. *R. Blaisdell photo & Collection*

173

A Tribute to the
Monterey Bay Aquarium

A New Chapter Begins on Cannery Row

Even though there have been many changes on Cannery Row since the day of the sardine, among the biggest—and certainly one of the most significant—was the birth of the fabulous Monterey Bay Aquarium. From its opening in 1984 through September, 2009, the aquarium welcomed more than 46 million visitors, or nearly two million per year. Just as impressively, thousands of volunteers donated nearly three million hours of service to help welcome and educate the guests who flocked to see the facility.

Known and respected throughout the world for the quality of its exhibits, its cutting-edge research, and its efforts on behalf of ocean conservation, the aquarium is routinely ranked as the number one institution of its kind in the United States. Certainly, its founding and growth have been a major part of the revival of Cannery Row.

It is with this in mind, coupled with the fact that 2009—the year this book was revised—marks the aquarium's twenty-fifth anniversary, that I decided to end this work with a look back at its first quarter century. Here, then, is a brief tribute to the Monterey Bay Aquarium, along with a wish for its continued success in the years to come.

If anyone had any doubt, once people saw a 43-foot-long whale being trucked down Cannery Row, the rumor of an aquarium coming to town was confirmed. Today this fiberglass model of a female gray whale hangs from the ceiling of the aquarium's Marine Mammal Hall. *Monterey Bay Aquarium Collection*

If it weren't for the automobiles, it would be hard to believe that these two photos were taken more than forty years apart (the inset photo is also shown on page 155). The similarity between the two pictures reflects the determination of the aquarium's founders to preserve the feel of the Hovden complex that originally occupied this site. Among the structures that were salvaged at least in part was the old warehouse building (left). Other features were replicated, such as selected smokestacks that were replaced by ones made out of fiber-glass. The entrance is shown at the center of the main photo (circa 1987). *Monterey Bay Aquarium Collection; inset, Hathaway Collection*

From a short distance away one gets a different view of the Monterey Bay Aquarium, which lines both sides of Cannery Row (circa 1990). *R. Reinstedt photo & Collection*

As time marched on, so too did the Monterey Bay Aquarium—right down Cannery Row (photo circa 2000). The citizens of Monterey (and beyond) are delighted with the prosperity and prestige the facility has brought to the Peninsula, and are proud that it has chosen Monterey and its beautiful bay as its home. *R. Reinstedt photo & Collection*

In addition to their primary goal of inspiring conservation of the oceans, the dedicated members of the aquarium's staff are also interested in sharing the colorful history of Cannery Row and its immediate environs with the visiting public. One way they accomplish this is through a series of strategically placed information kiosks. The one shown here, "From Sardines to a Sanctuary," tells the story of Cannery Row from the 1920s through the establishment of the Monterey Bay National Marine Sanctuary in 1992. *R. Reinstedt photo & Collection*

Long before the aquarium worked its way down Cannery Row, many of the ramshackle buildings that lined the street's north shore (in addition to those that were part of the original Hovden plant) were acquired and demolition began. Events such as these were made possible by David and Lucile Packard and helped set the stage for construction. Above we see part of the original cannery site as construction began. The large white building near the center of the photo is the Hovden warehcuse. The skeleton-type structure to its right (foreground) houses boiler room equipment salvaged from the cannery. *Monterey Bay Aquarium Collection*

In looking toward the bay we get a different view of the carefully covered boiler room equipment. Along the way the equipment was restored and became part of the aquarium's main entrance exhibit (inset). Among other things, this exhibit offers visitors a nostalgic look at the Hovden plant, a peek at old Cannery Row, a glimpse into the Marine Biological Laboratory—and home—of Ed "Doc" Ricketts (of Steinbeck fame), and interactive displays that contain information about such things as the sardine canning process. *Monterey Bay Aquarium Collection*

Monterey Bay Aquarium Collection

As construction progressed, the aquarium slowly began to take shape, as these views from Cannery Row show. Easily recognizable, the original Hovden warehouse is at the left of each photo. *Monterey Bay Aquarium Collection*

183

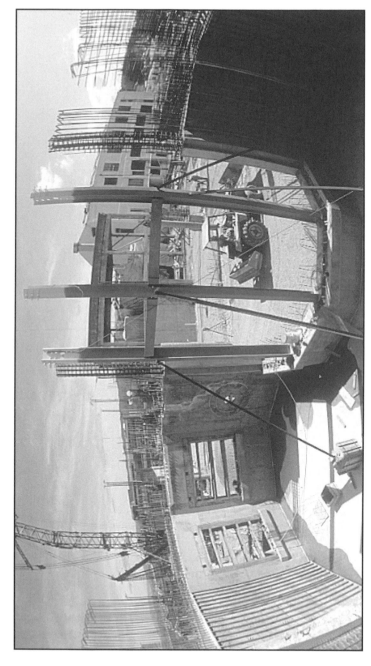

Looking through the skeleton of the future Kelp Forest exhibit, we again see the Hovden warehouse in the distance. *Monterey Bay Aquarium Collection*

The Kelp Forest soon became one of the aquarium's most popular exhibits. The diver helps to bring perspective to the picture as he inspects the tank, feeds the fish, monitors the kelp, and keeps a watchful eye on the abundance of marine life that thrives in the habitat. *Monterey Bay Aquarium Collection*

Divers get a real workout when it's window-washing day in the Kelp Forest. Recognized as the world's first living kelp forest exhibit, the tank stretches to three stories in height and contains more than 340,000 gallons of seawater. Although countless forms of sea life inhabit the exhibit, the stars of the show are the giant kelp, a type of seaweed. The 100-plus varieties that thrive in the tank include species that are among the fastest-growing plants in the world. *Monterey Bay Aquarium Collection*

186

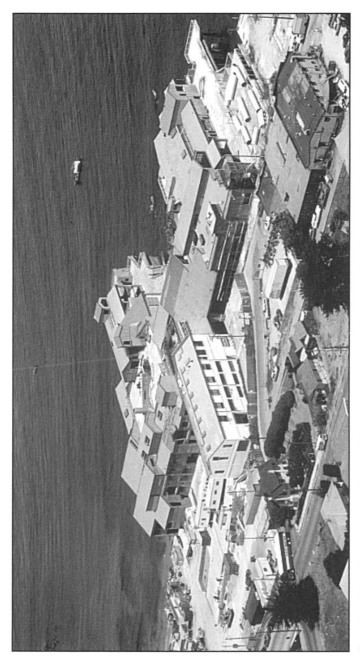

Even though the Kelp Forest and other exhibits were completed long before opening day, work continued at a frenzied pace as the long-anticipated day approached. Visible in this view is the now-familiar Hovden warehouse (the large white building) as well as the aquarium's overall design. *Monterey Bay Aquarium Collection*

Finally, the great day arrived! Here we see Julie Packard, Executive Director of the Monterey Bay Aquarium, flanked by her proud parents, Lucile and David, during the opening day ceremonies on October 20, 1984. *Monterey Bay Aquarium Collection*

The line was long, and the people were in a festive mood, as the Monterey Bay Aquarium opened its doors to the public at last. Prominent in the foreground (left) is the original Hovden warehouse, while in the distance (at the junction of David Avenue and Cannery Row) we see a portion of the aquarium's original entryway. *Monterey Bay Aquarium Collection*

As captivating as it was during the day, the aquarium was, perhaps, even more magical at night, as opening day festivities continued into the dark. *Monterey Bay Aquarium Collection*

Many agreed that the new Monterey Bay Aquarium was an especially striking sight when viewed from the sea. *Monterey Bay Aquarium Collection*

The new aquarium was perhaps most impressive of all when seen from the air. *Monterey Bay Aquarium Collection*

Monterey Bay Aquarium Collection

The top photo shows part of the center court and deck area as seen from inside the aquarium. Beyond the court, and to the left of the extended deck (near the center of the picture) is the Great Tide Pool, an aquarium favorite for both visitors and the creatures that inhabit it. In the bottom photo, looking toward the Ocean's Edge wing (from the vicinity of the extended deck) we get a better view of the tide pool. *Monterey Bay Aquarium Collection*

Young and old alike thrill to a wave crashing over them as they explore the Ocean's Edge wing. Among the many displays in the Splash Zone galleries, created especially for kids and families, you'll find animals and their homes in the coral reef and rocky shores exhibits. Other highlights include black-footed penguins from South America, numerous hands-on activities, and a variety of interactive programs. *Monterey Bay Aquarium Collection*

With countless creatures, algae (sea-weeds), and plants big and small calling the Ocean's Edge wing home, it's hard to pick a favorite. However, there was a time during my frequent visits to the aquarium when I made a beeline for the Junk Tank to see the Sarcastic Fringe-head that lived in a bottle there. Yes, that's the creature's real name, and its home really is called the Junk Tank. In addition to this large-jawed fish and several of its marine friends, the exhibit includes a siz-able collection of junk one might find at the bottom of the sea. *Monterey Bay Aquarium Collection*

More than 550 different kinds of critters—numbering well over 35,000 individual specimens—inhabit the Monterey Bay Aquarium. Some of the most popular attractions, such as the lovable sea otter, the giant octopus, and the awe-inspiring jellyfish (which come in an assortment of shapes, sizes, and colors), have exhibits all their own. Other displays are home to a vast variety of creatures that dwell in the deep. And I mustn't forget the aviary, where visitors can see many kinds of birds that are associated with the sea. *Monterey Bay Aquarium Collection*

Monterey Bay Aquarium Collection

Monterey Bay Aquarium Collection

The great white shark (center of photo above) has captured the imagination of most anyone with an interest in beasts of the deep. The Monterey Bay Aquarium, which has become one of the leading authorities on shark behavior and conservation, holds the record for keeping a great white in captivity. The aquarium's awe-inspiring Outer Bay wing (completed in 1996) provides just the right environment to accommodate the needs of this amazing animal. Its main tank measures more than fifty-six feet wide and seventeen feet high, and holds more than one million gallons of seawater. Other than great whites, the tank is home to numerous other open-ocean animals, including tuna, hammerhead sharks, black sea turtles, sunfish, barracuda, sardines, and stingrays. We get a closer look at a great white on the facing page. *Monterey Bay Aquarium Collection*

Monterey Bay Aquarium Collection

With this aerial view of the aquarium as it appeared after completion of the Outer Bay wing, we bring our twenty-fifth anniversary tribute to a close (the Outer Bay wing is to the left). Looking to the future, we can only hope that the Monterey Bay Aquarium will continue to instill in visitors a desire to help preserve the vast natural resources of our oceans—a goal that is even more vital today than when this amazing facility first opened its doors on Cannery Row a quarter of a century ago. *Monterey Bay Aquarium Collection*

Acknowledgments

As with several of my other books, it is difficult to acknowledge each and every person who donated time, told a tale, tracked down information, loaned photographs, opened a family album, diary, or scrapbook, or, sometimes most important of all, simply had an encouraging word to say. Without these people, and their willingness to share their memories and mementos, this book could not have been written, and it is to them that much of the credit for this work should be given.

Speaking of credit, I would like to note that all of the photographs have been credited to the source from which they came. When known, the photographer's name is also included. Certainly, it is the photographers, known and unknown, whose interest and involvement in Monterey's waterfront have made this pictorial history possible.

Among the many people who have contributed photographs or information, I would like to single out and thank Lee Blaisdell, Robert Blaisdell, Vincent J. Bruno, Gaspar V. Cardinale, Vincent Colletto, John "Bricky" Crivello, John N. Crivello, Anita M. Ferrante, Salvatore A. Ferrante, Ruth Fisher, Kevin Ford, James A. Gruber, Pat Hathaway, Chris Ingram, Don Livermore, Dominic Mineo, Frank J. Nuovo, Werner Papenhoefer, Dorothy Ronald, Marilyn Rodrock, Tom R. Russo, Jessie Sandholdt, Mary Sherman, Tony R. Souza, Admiral Earl E. Stone, and Jack Stracuzzi.

A special tip of the mariner's cap is due to the late Allen Knight. As the photo credits indicate, many of the photographs in this book originally came from what was then known as the Allen Knight Maritime Museum Collection. The collection was donated to the Monterey History & Art Association by Allen's widow, Adele Knight, in 1970. Today it is known as the Monterey Maritime & History Collection.

Along the way countless other people have expressed interest, added their comments or corrections, introduced me to old-timers, and in many other ways contributed to the success of this book. To all these people, and especially to my editor, John Bergez, I extend my heartfelt thanks.

And, finally, I owe my greatest thanks to all the rest of the Reinstedts. This work would not exist without the support of my wife, Debbie, who put up with me from the writing of the original work to its revision thirty-plus years later, and my son, Erick, who became an indispensable partner in the production of this edition, scanning pictures, typesetting the text, and offering countless suggestions and words of encouragement along the way. And to Mary Ann, Bethany, and Abigail, what can I say except thank you for sharing your husband, father, and house with me as Erick and I holed up in his office until we had tweaked the last picture, typed the last word, and finally put this book to bed for the last time.

Books by Randall A. Reinstedt

Regional History and Lore Series . . .
bringing the colorful history of California's Central Coast to life for adults and older children

California Ghost Notes
From Fisherman's Wharf to Steinbeck's Cannery Row
Ghost Notes
Ghostly Tales and Mysterious Happenings of Old Monterey
Ghosts, Bandits and Legends of Old Monterey
Ghosts and Mystery Along Old Monterey's Path of History
Ghosts of the Big Sur Coast
Incredible Ghosts of Old Monterey's Hotel Del Monte
Monterey's Mother Lode
Mysterious Sea Monsters of California's Central Coast
Shipwrecks and Sea Monsters of California's Central Coast
Tales, Treasures and Pirates of Old Monterey

History & Happenings of California Series . . .
putting the story back in history for young readers

Lean John, California's Horseback Hero
One-Eyed Charley, the California Whip
Otters, Octopuses, and Odd Creatures of the Deep
Stagecoach Santa
The Strange Case of the Ghosts of the
    Robert Louis Stevenson House
Tales and Treasures of California's Missions
Tales and Treasures of California's Ranchos
Tales and Treasures of the California Gold Rush

For information on purchasing books contact:

Ghost Town Publications
P.O. Drawer 5998 ✦ Carmel, CA 93921 ✦ (831) 373-2885
www.ghosttownpub.com